Legal

Copyright © 2019 Matthew L. Myers, CEO and Founder of Infrastructure Upgrade, Inc.® All Rights Reserved. Printed in the United States. Except as permitted under the United States Copyright Act of 1976, no part of this publication may be reproduced or distributed in any form or by any means, or stored in a data base, without prior permission of the publisher.

All drawings, illustrations and photographs are the legal property of the publishers Matthew L. Myers. Copyright © 2019 Matthew L. Myers. All Rights Reserved.

Infrastructure Upgrade® is registered Trademark of the U.S. Patent & Trademark Office (USPTO).

Sutter Law (based in San Francisco) provides legal services for Infrastructure Upgrade, Inc.®

ISBN: 978-1-7321877-3-3

This publication is designed to provide accurate and authoritative information in regard to the subject matter covered. It is sold with the understanding that neither the author nor the publisher is engaged in rendering legal, accounting, or other professional service. If legal advice or other expert assistance is required, the services of a competent professional person should be sought.

--From a Declaration of Principles Jointly Adopted by a Committee of the American Bar Association and a Committee of Publishers and Associations.

The views and opinions expressed herein are those of the author alone and do not reflect the views of any university, employers, former employers and/or their affiliates.

Table of Contents

Flipbook..4

Flipbook

The animation (below) was originally done as a stop action film, converted into Flash® and now is being published as a flipbook.

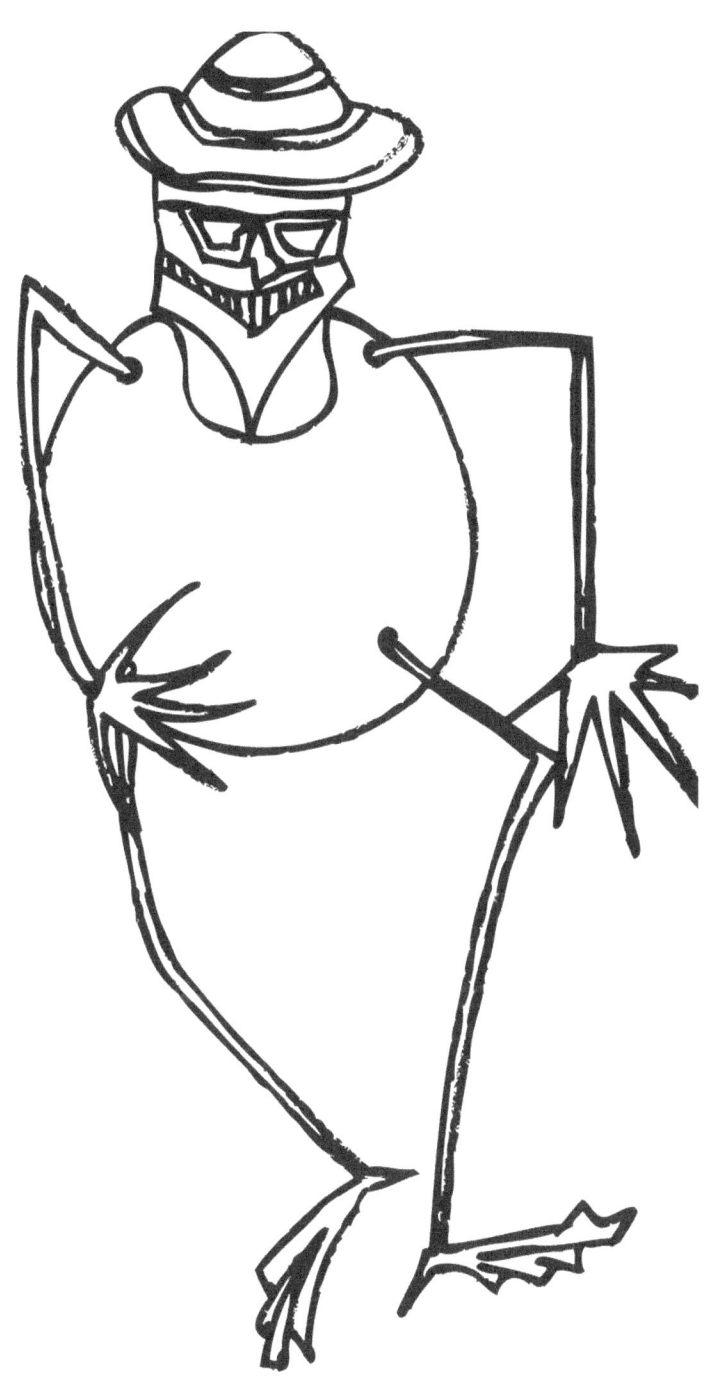

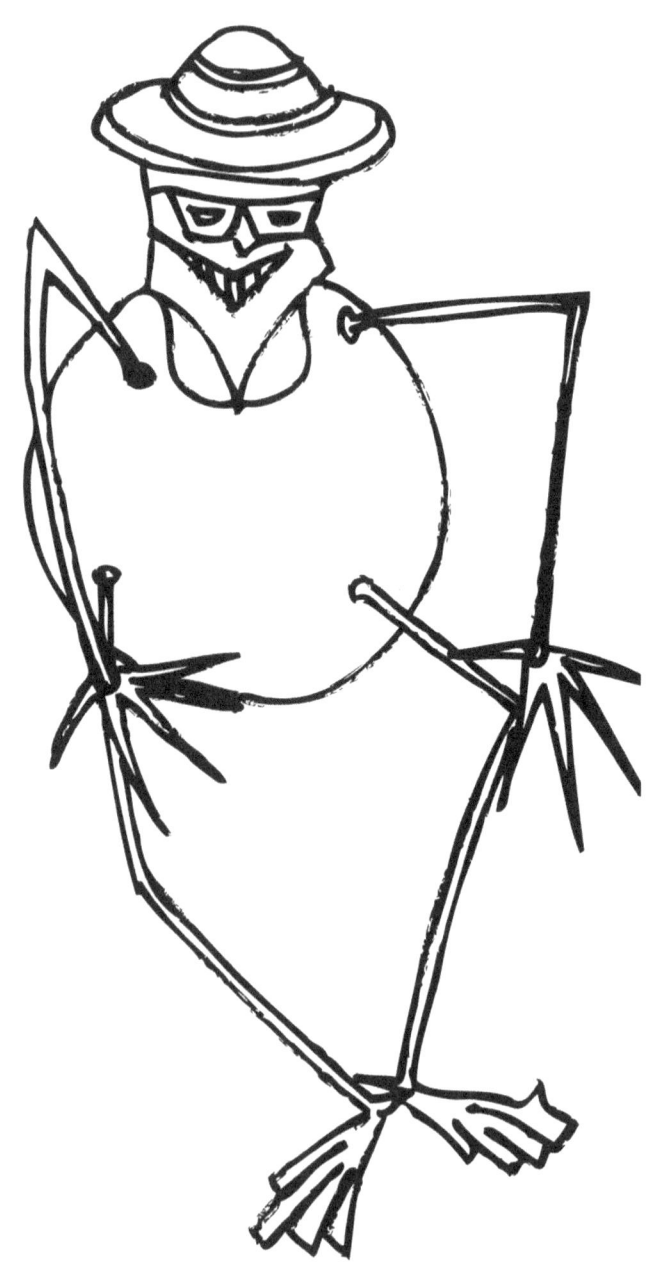

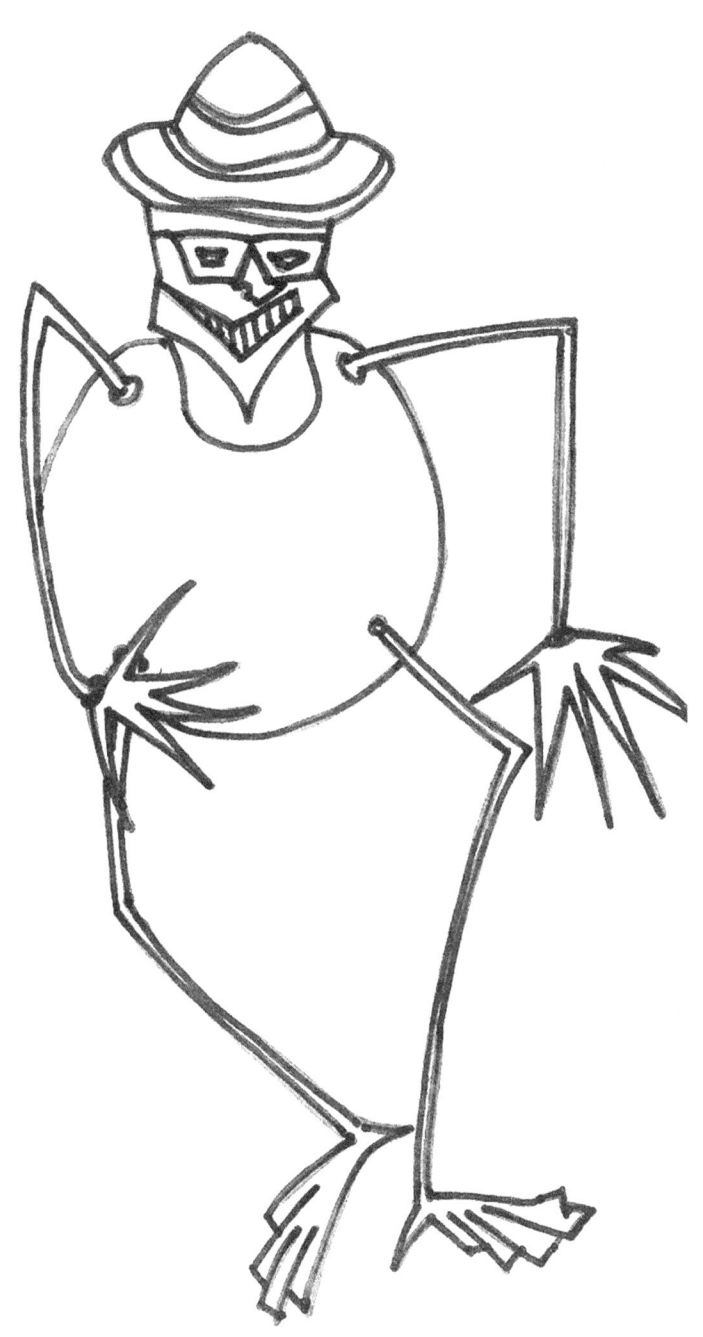

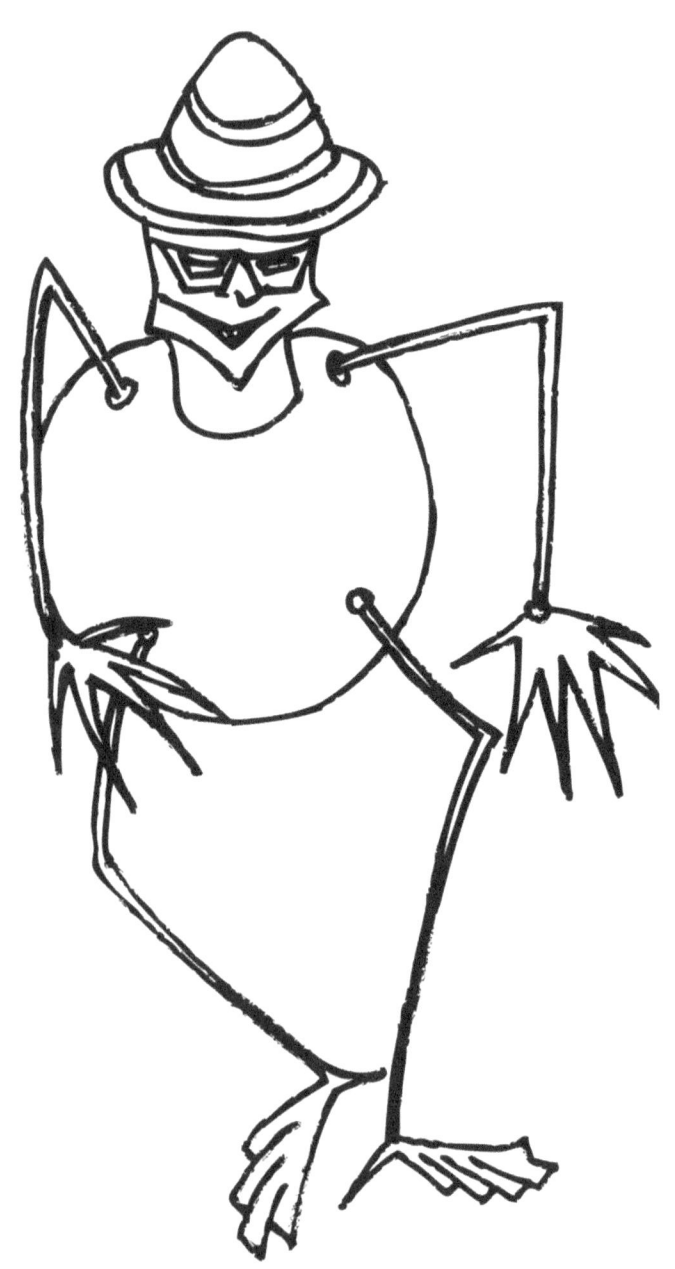

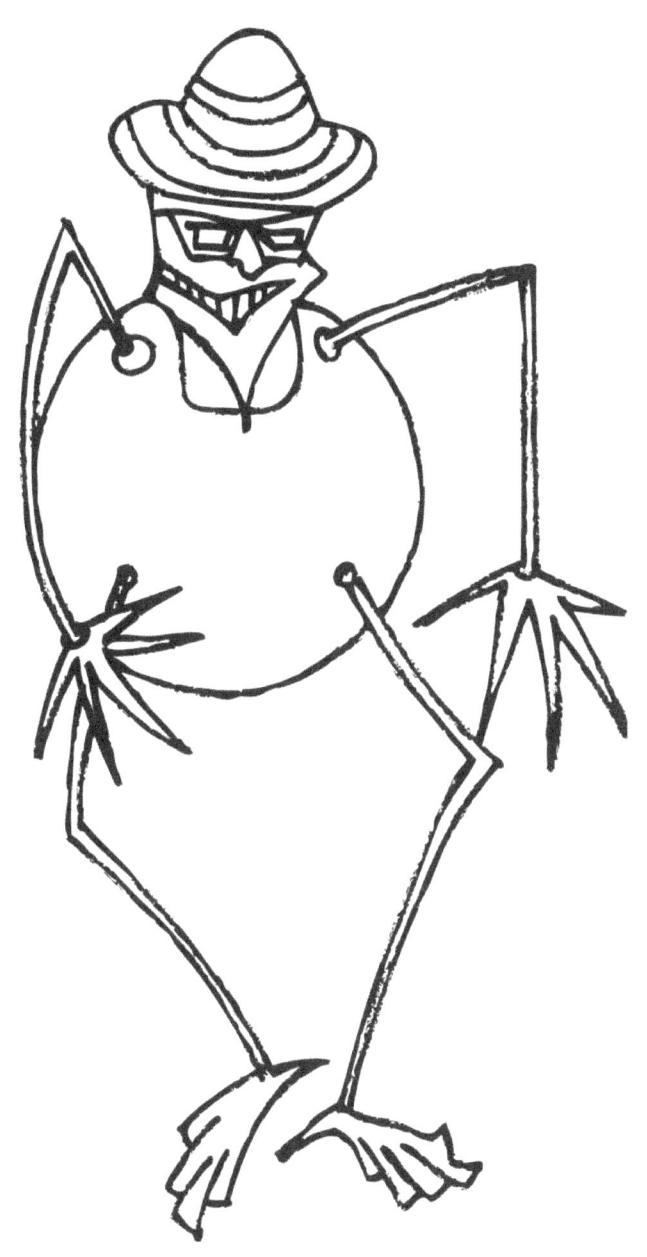

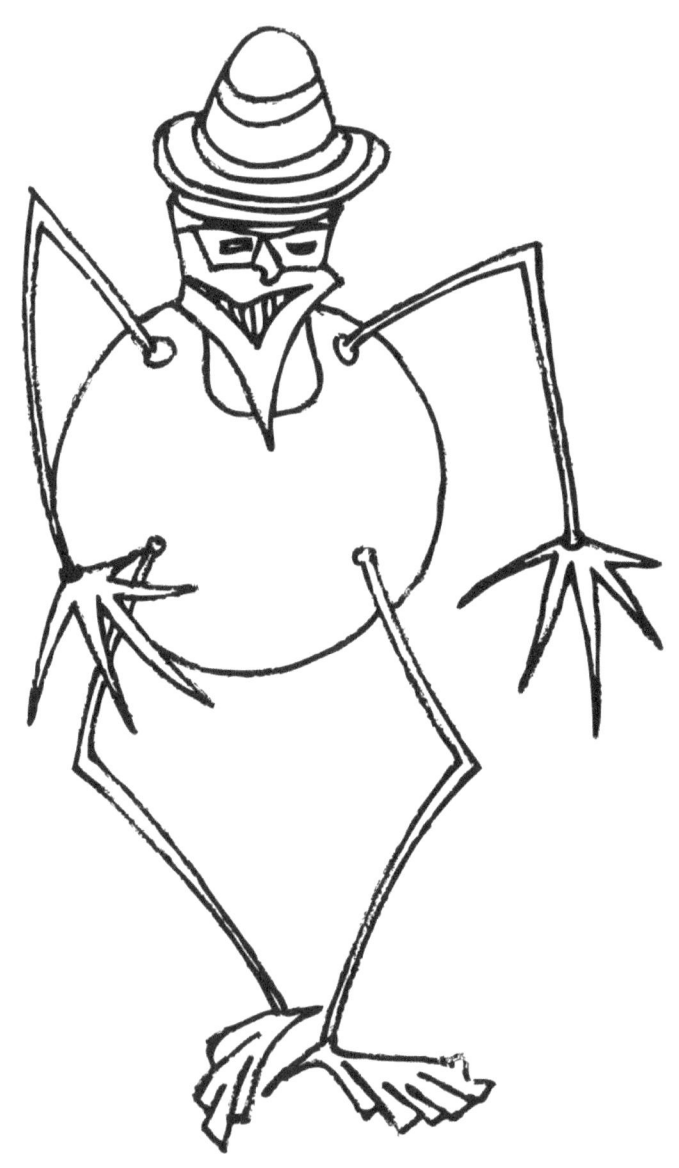

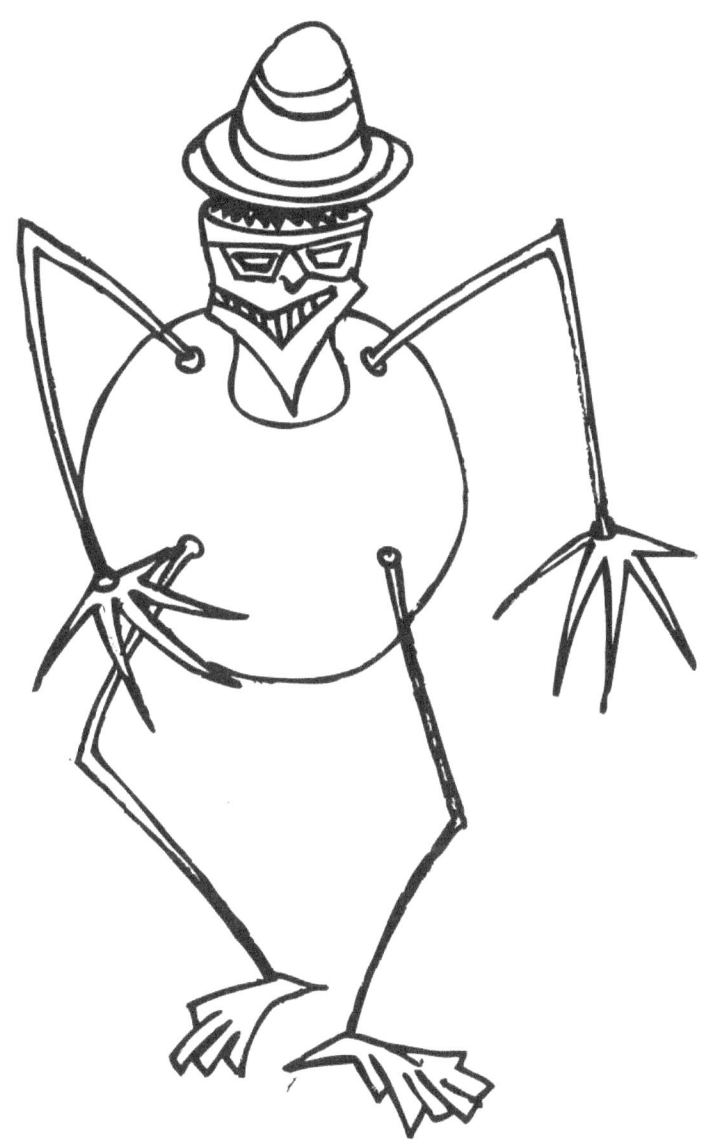

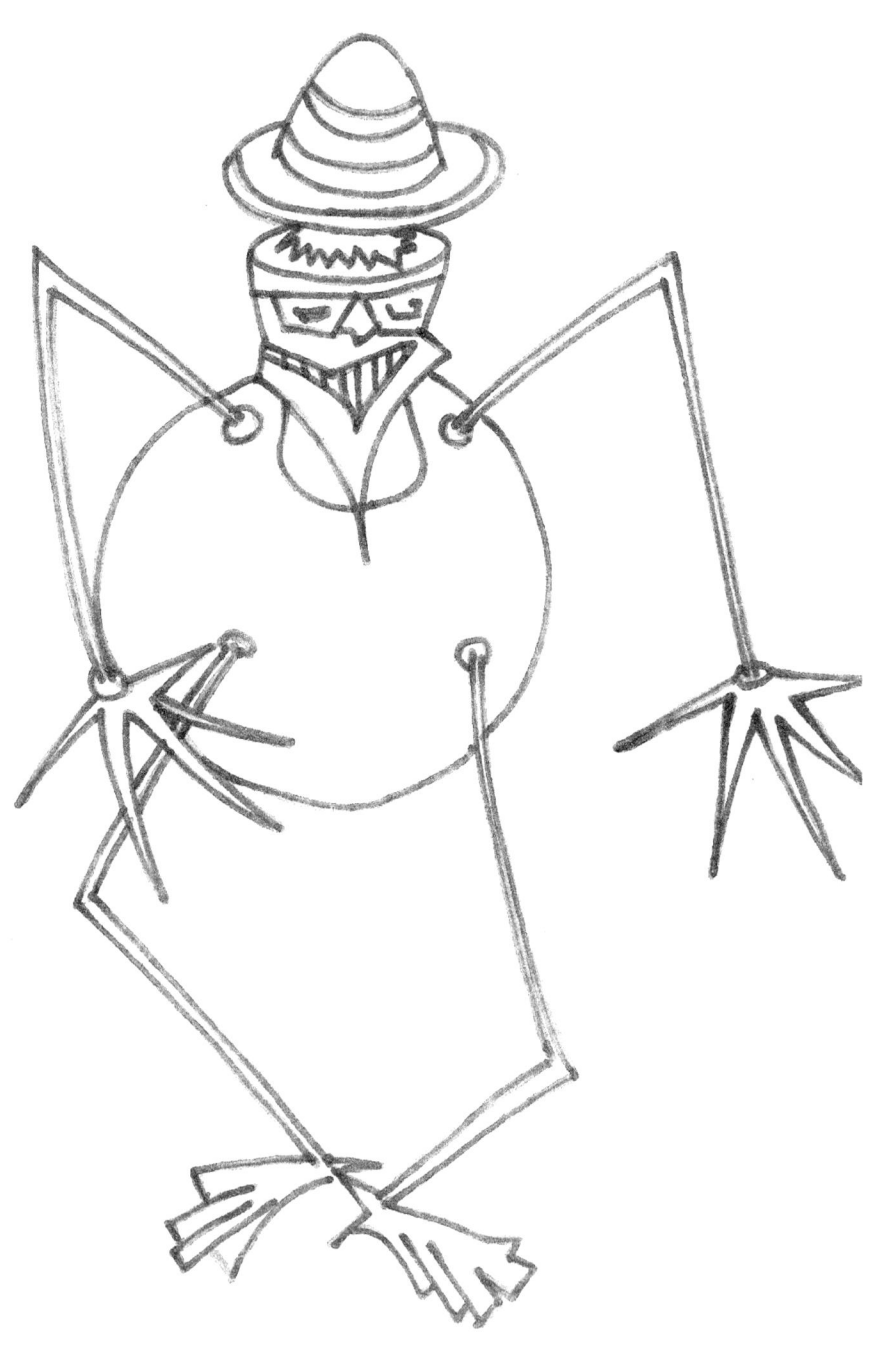

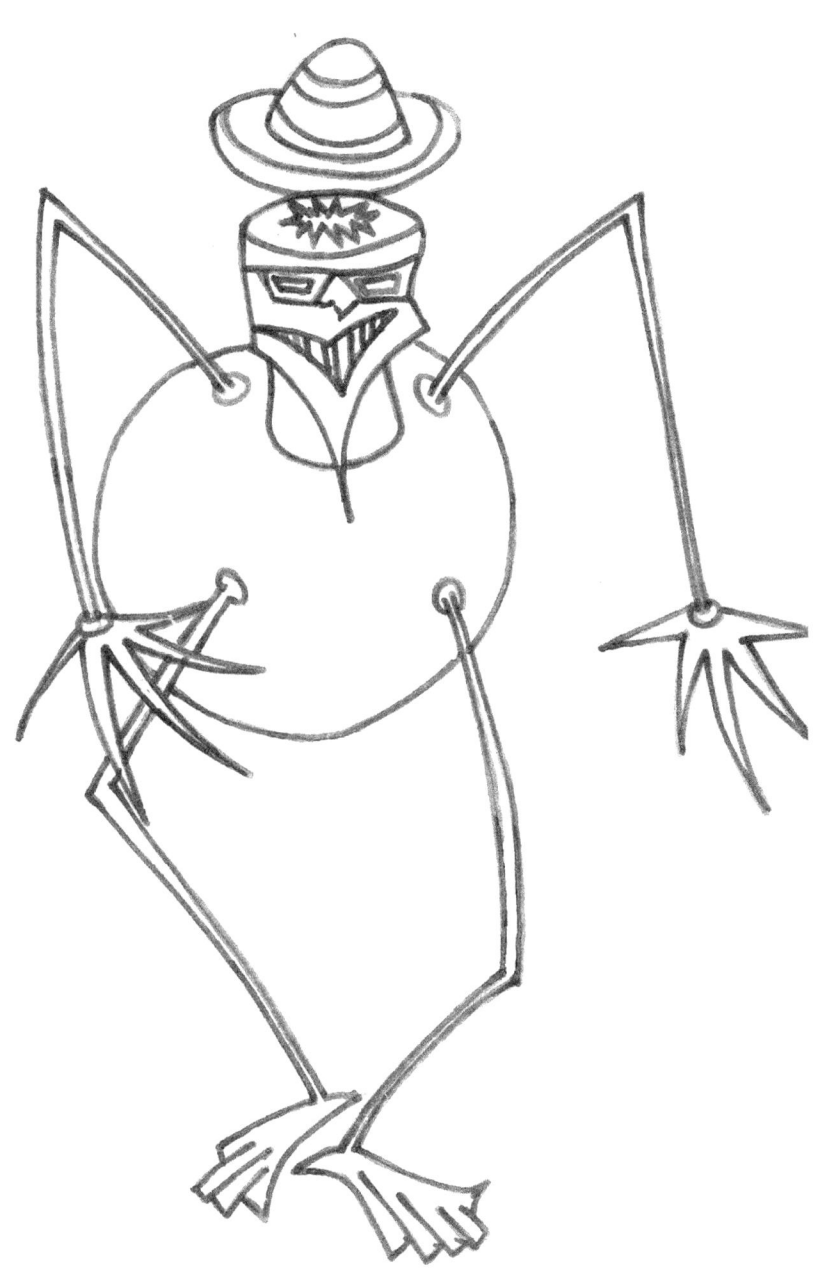

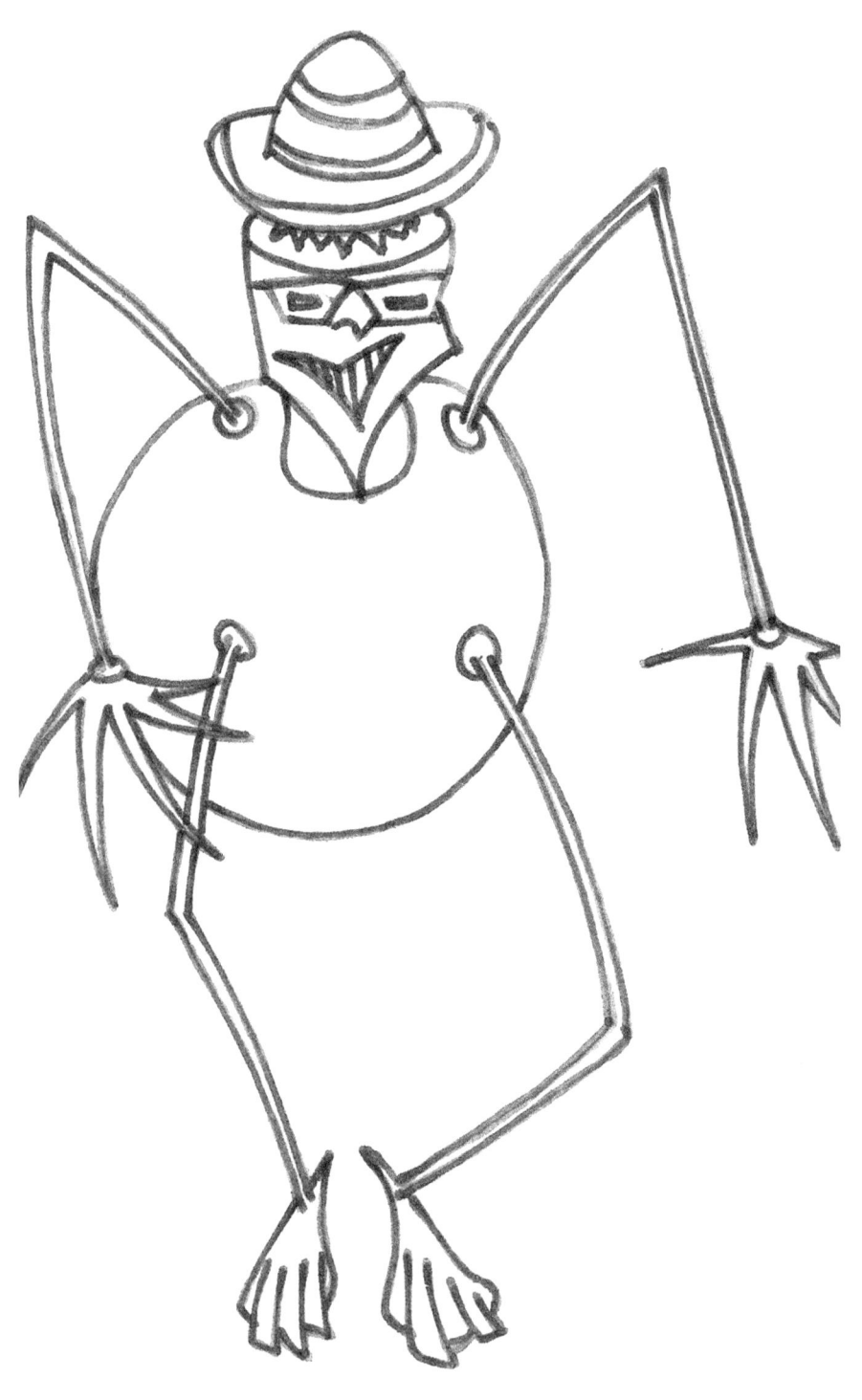

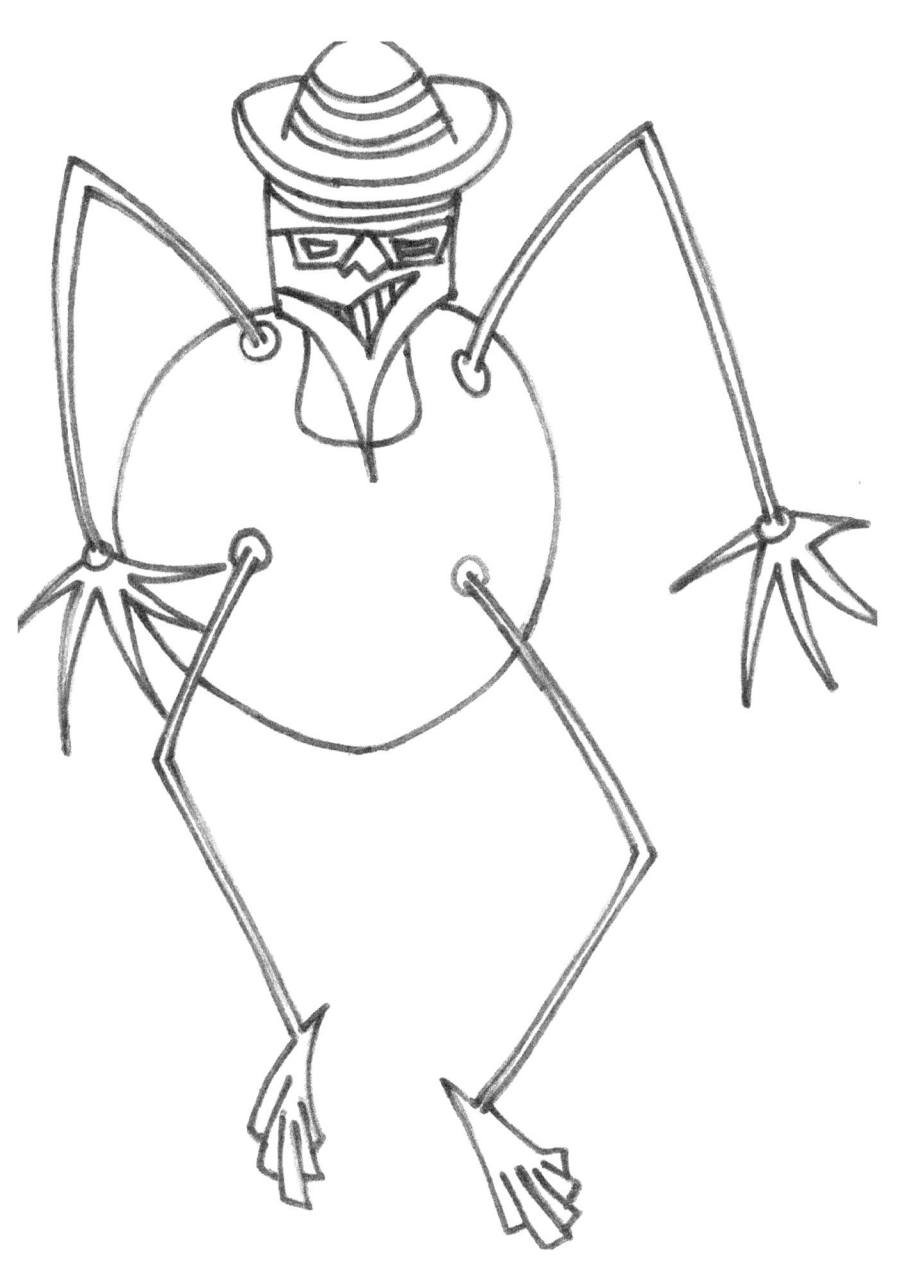

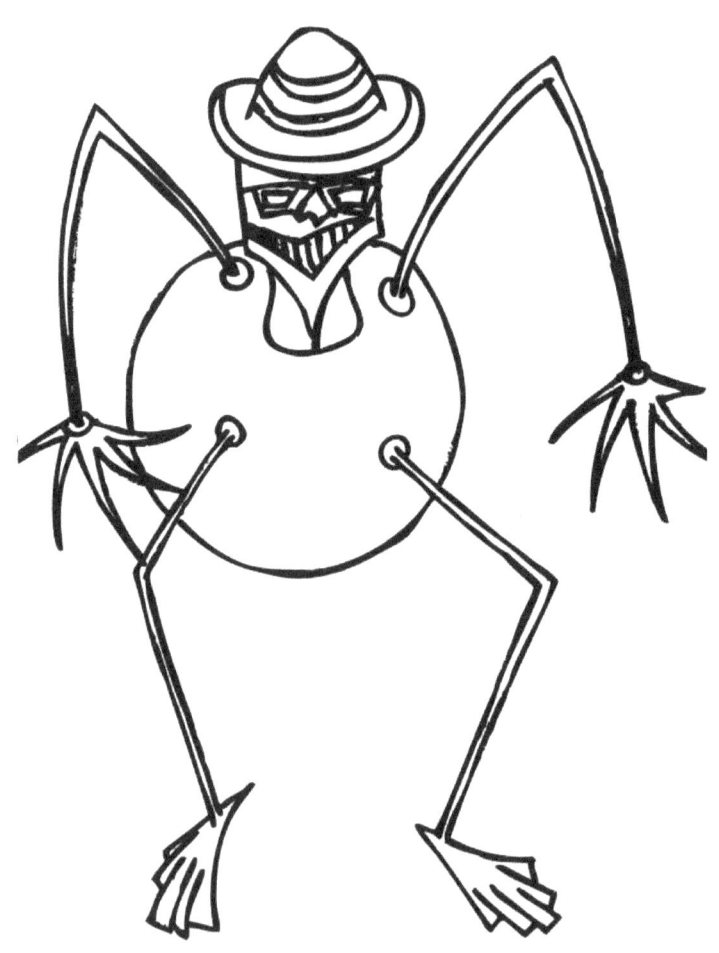

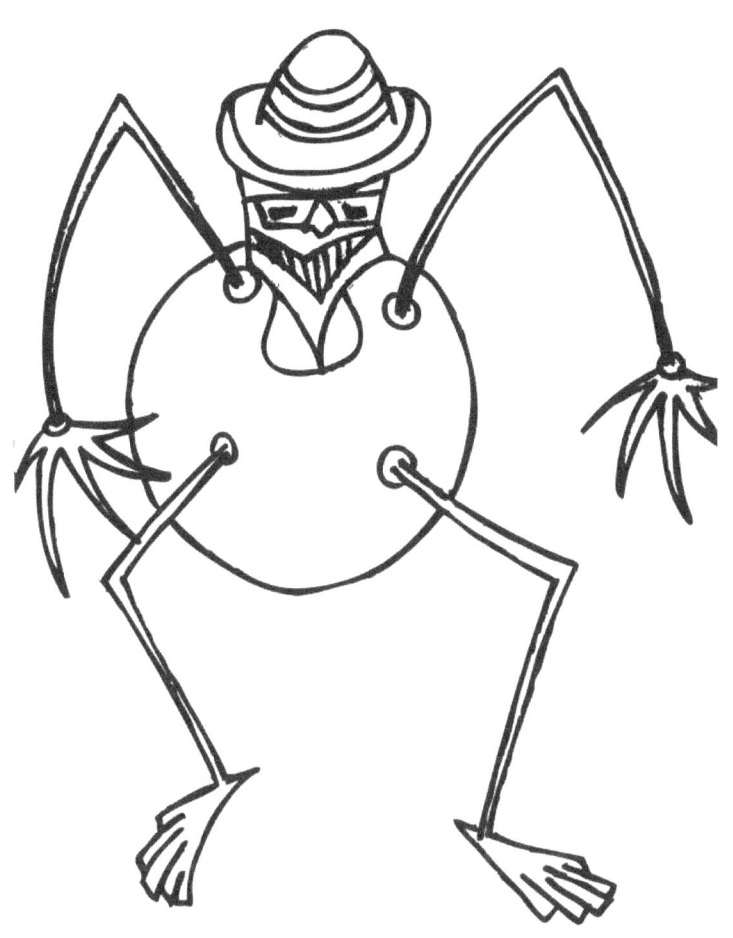

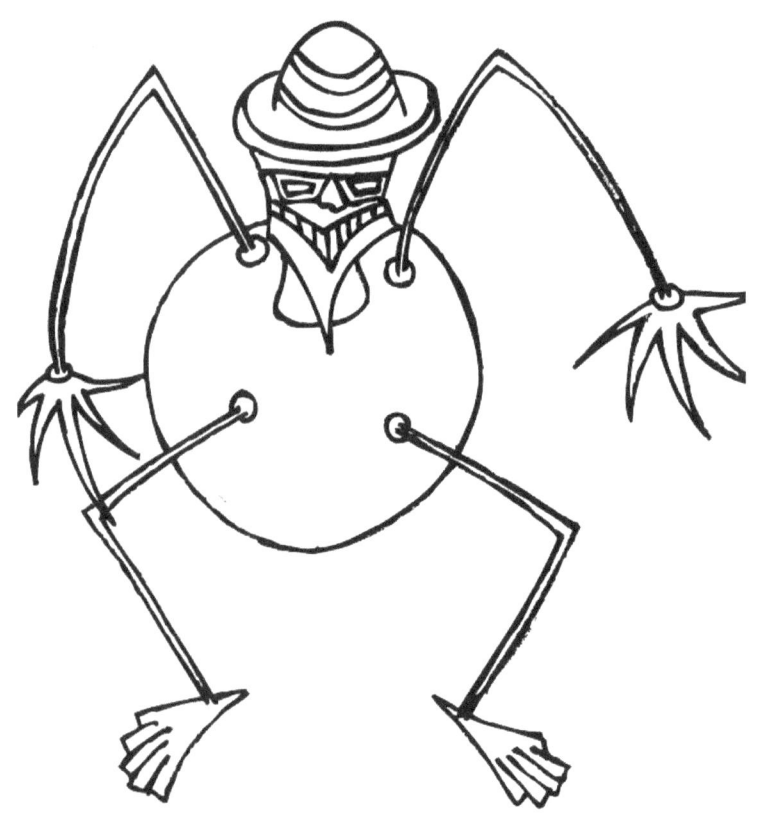

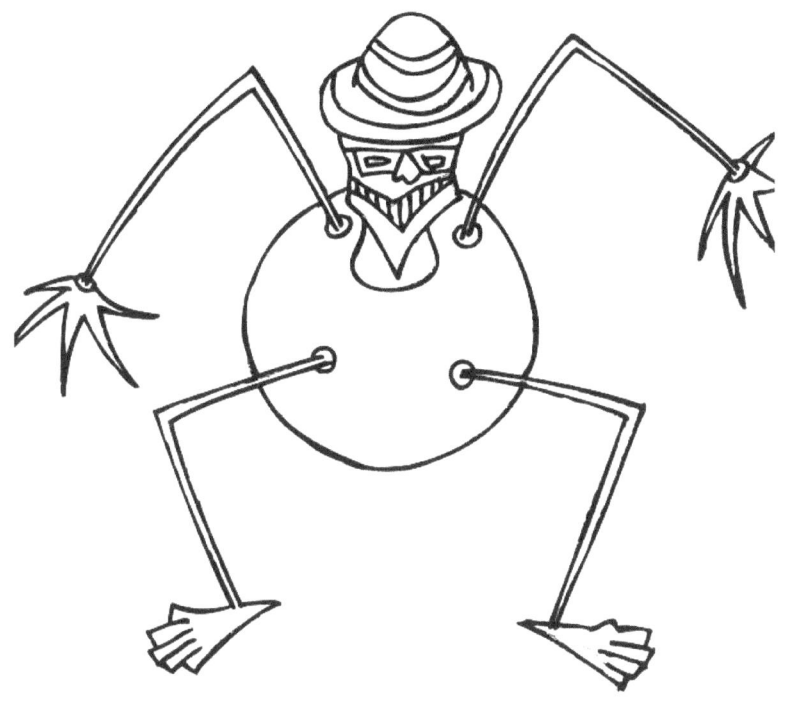

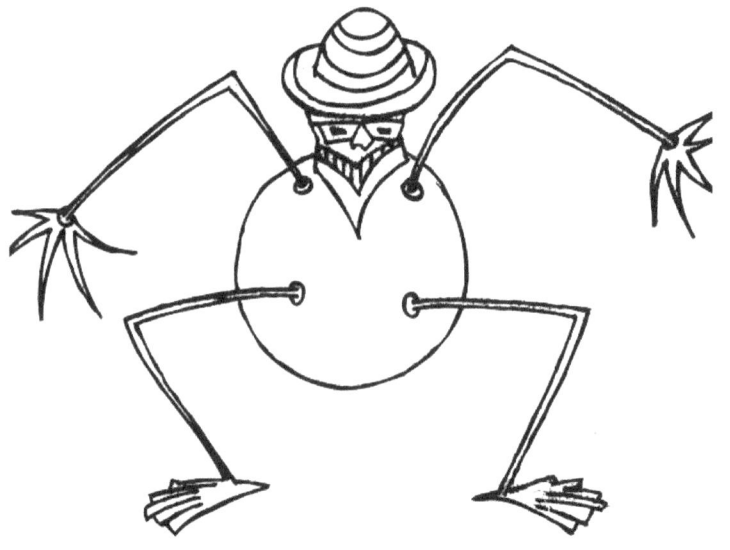

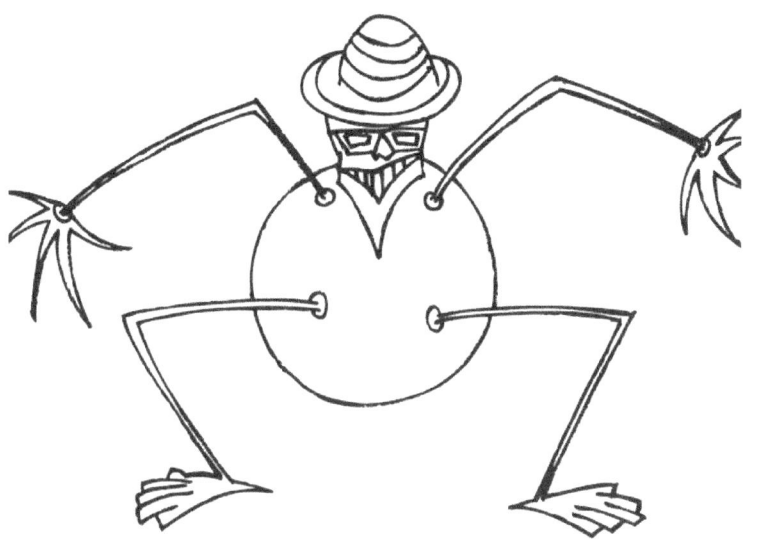

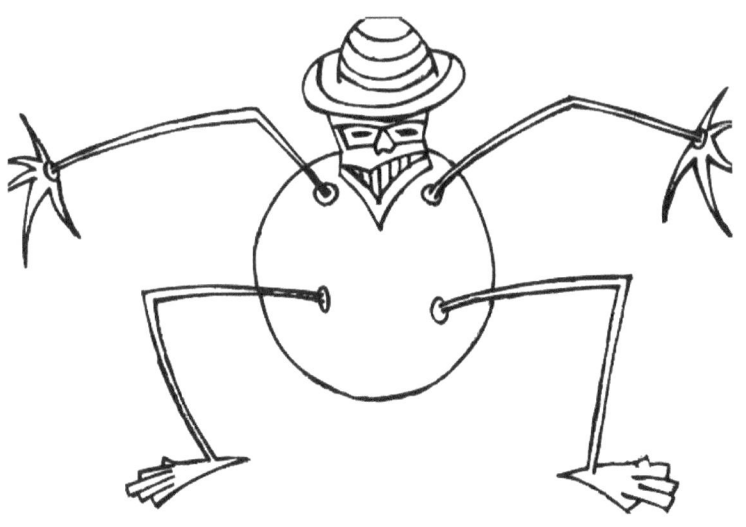

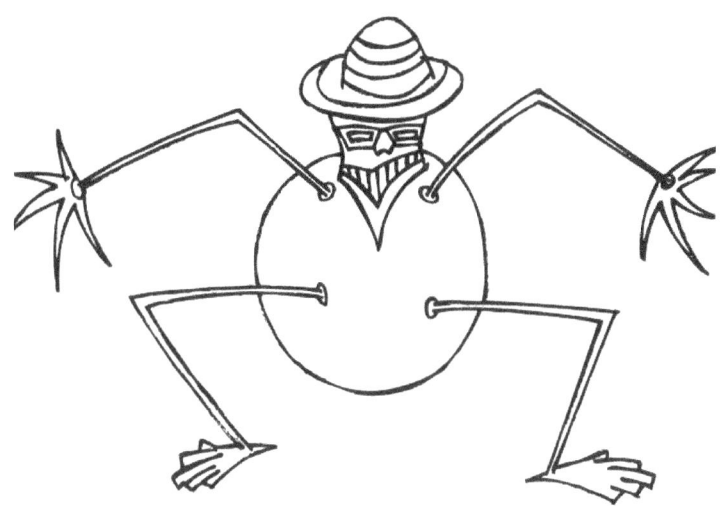

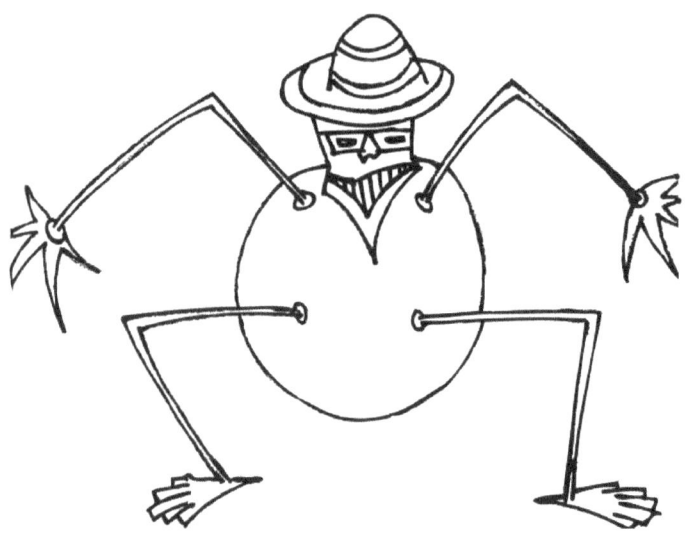

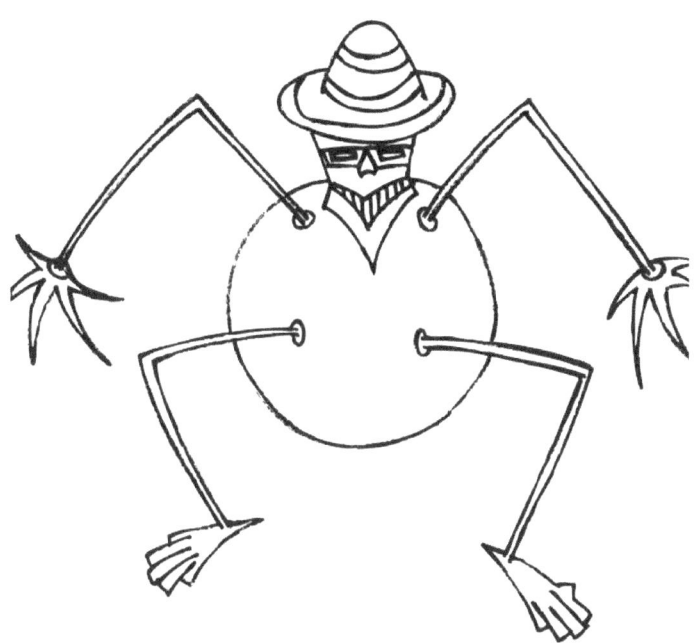

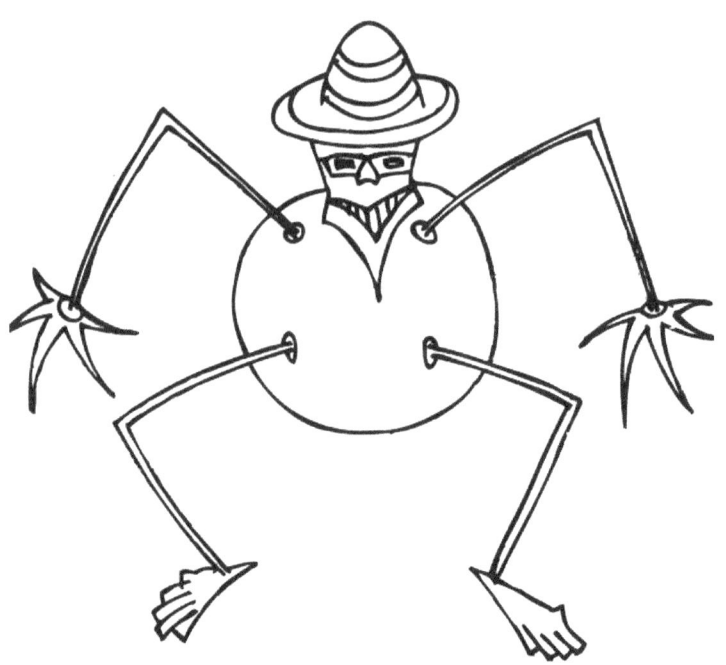

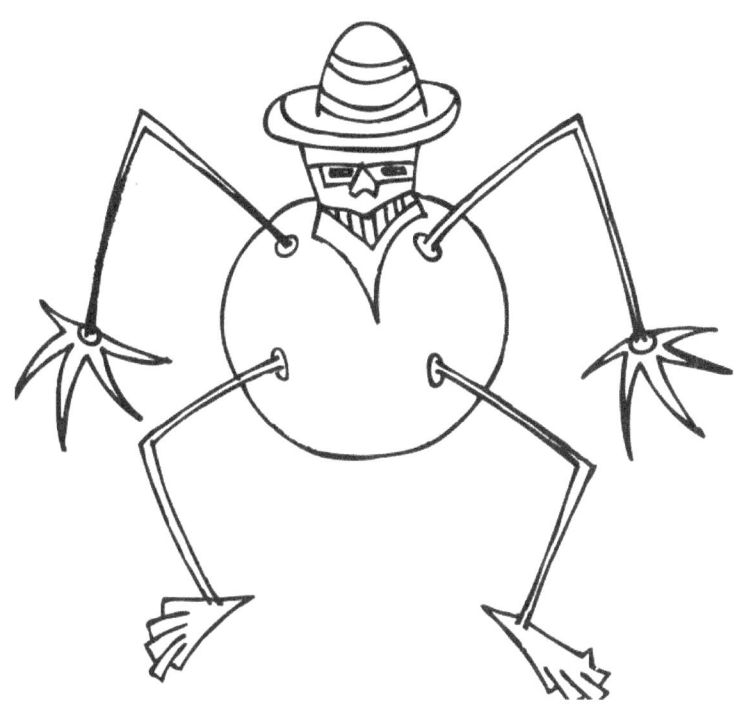

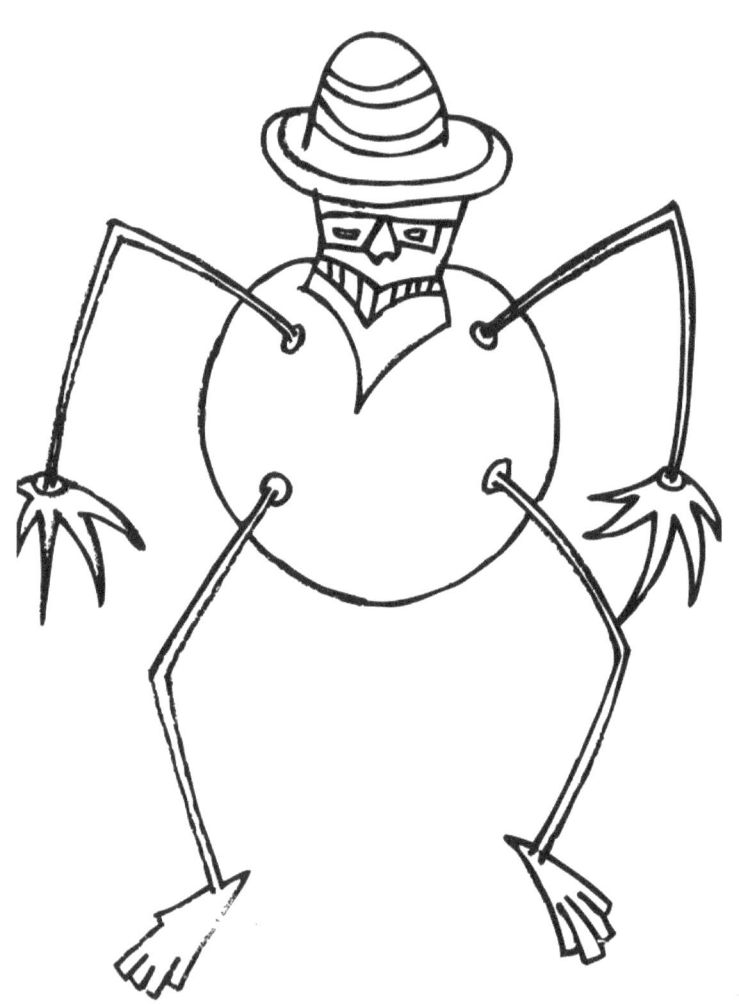

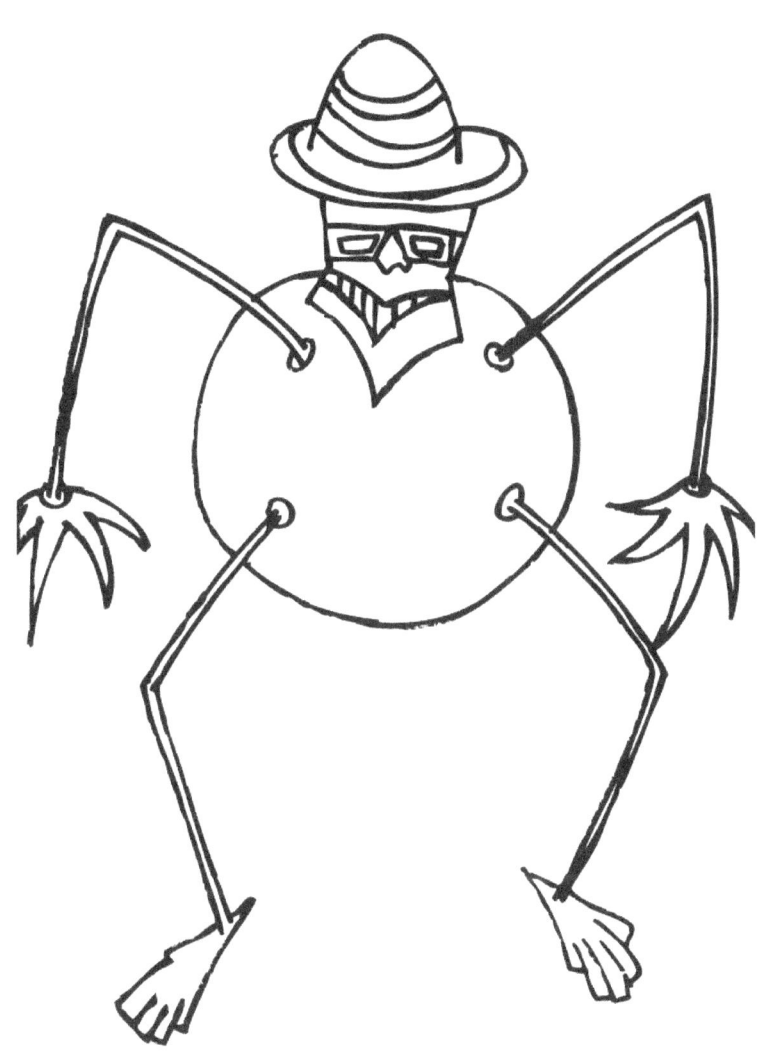

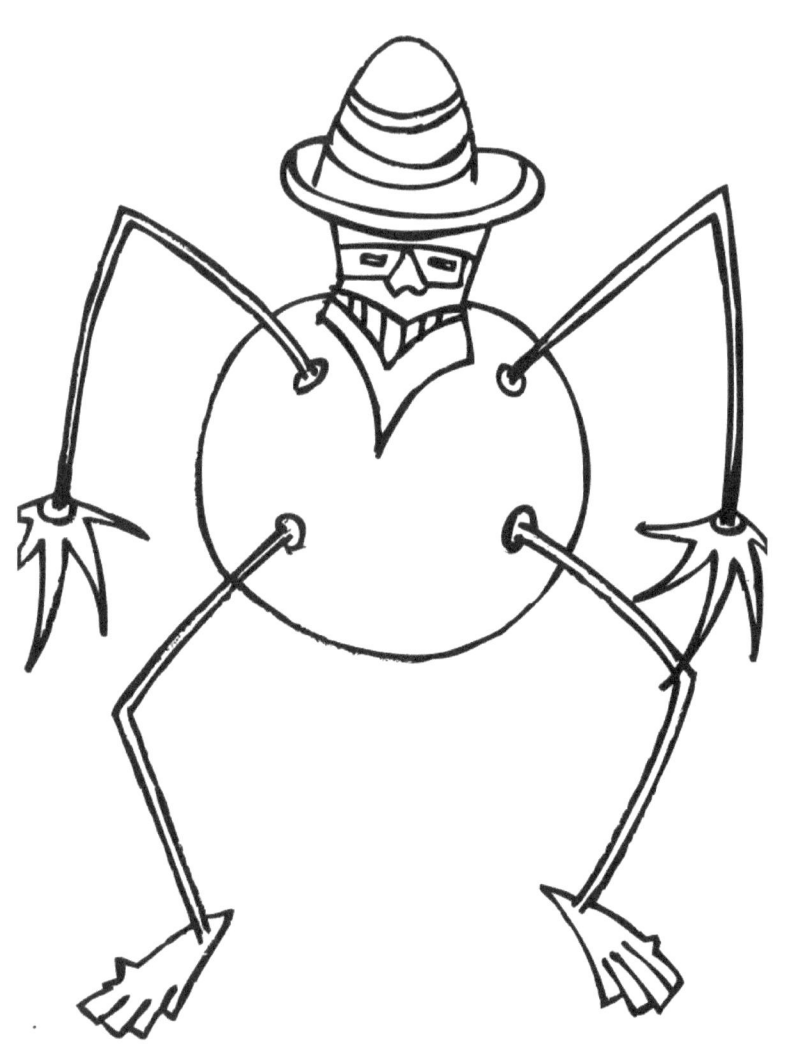

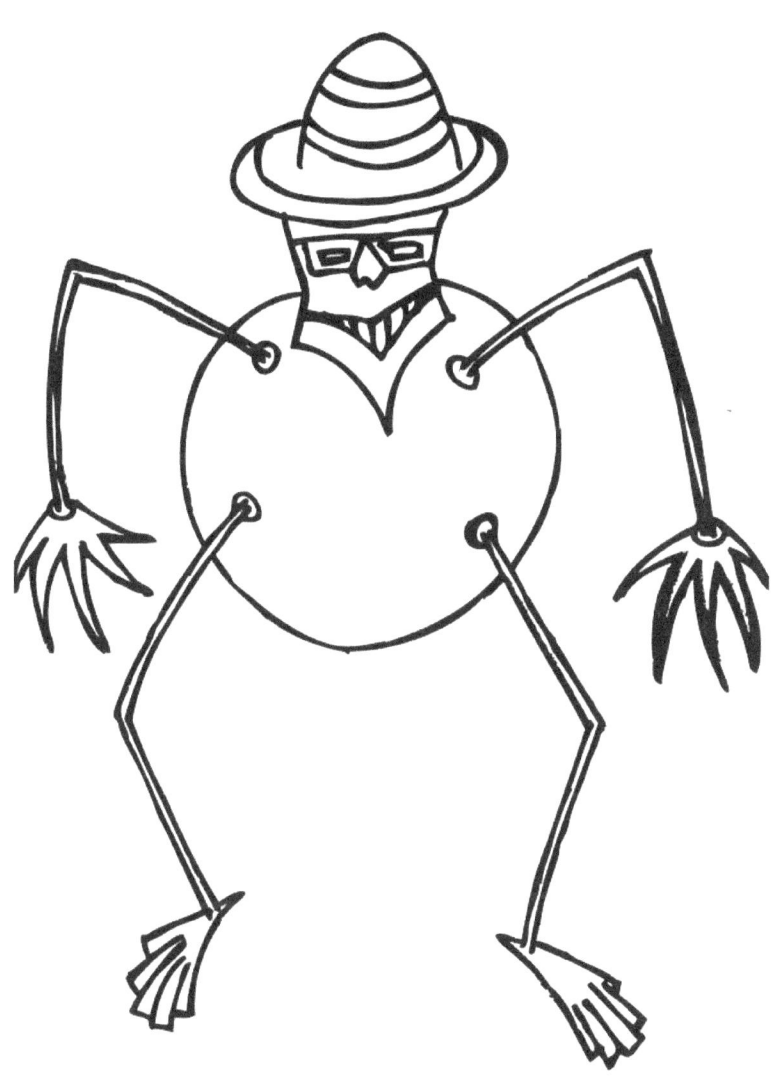

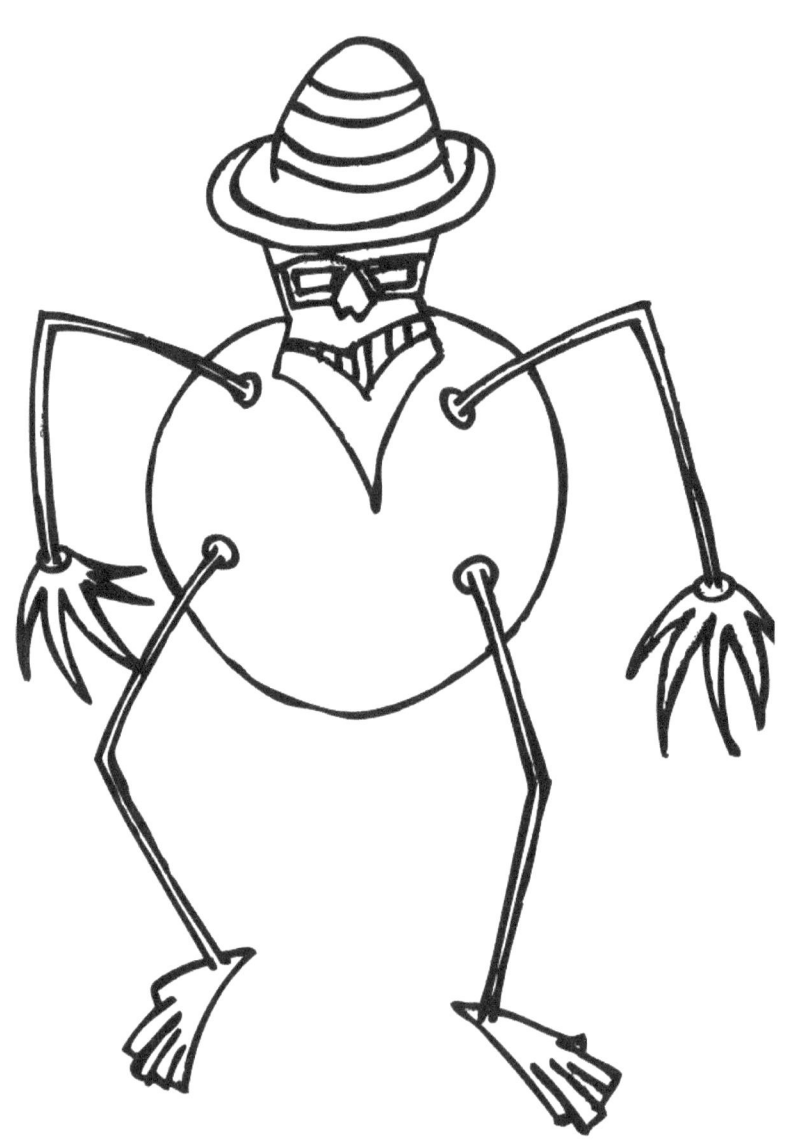

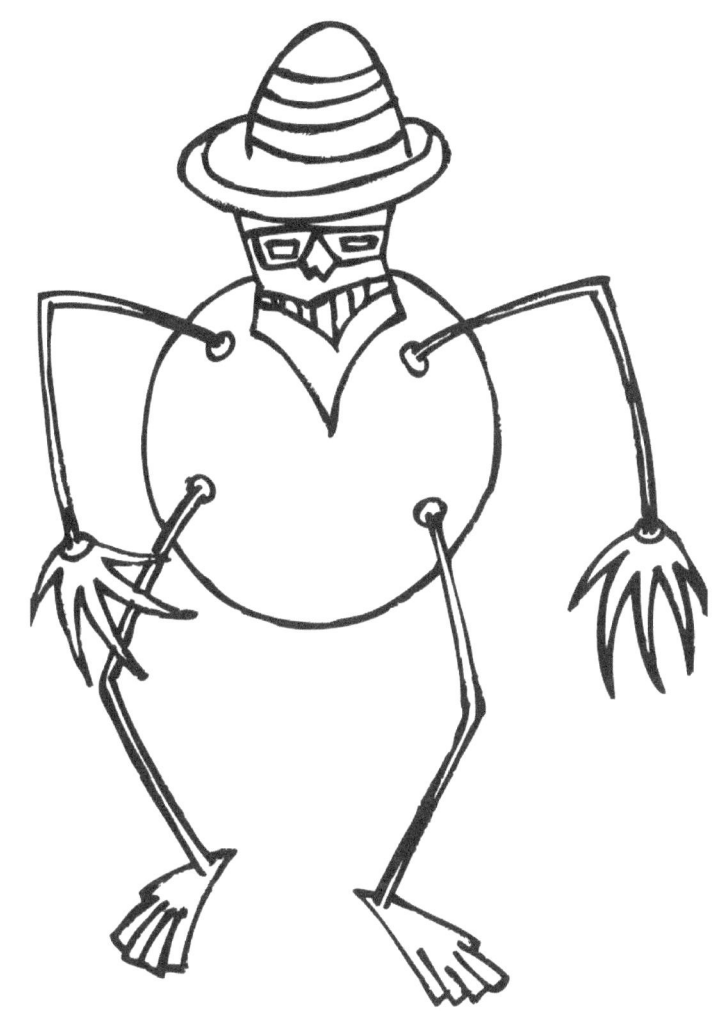

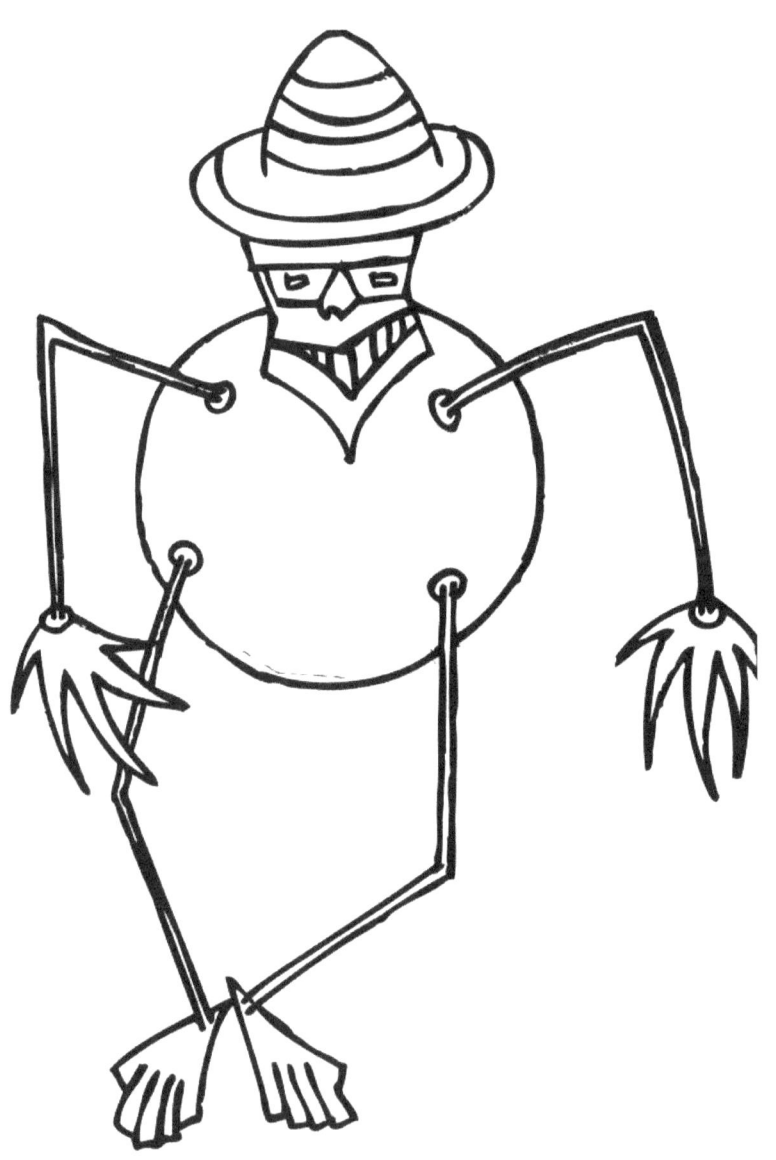

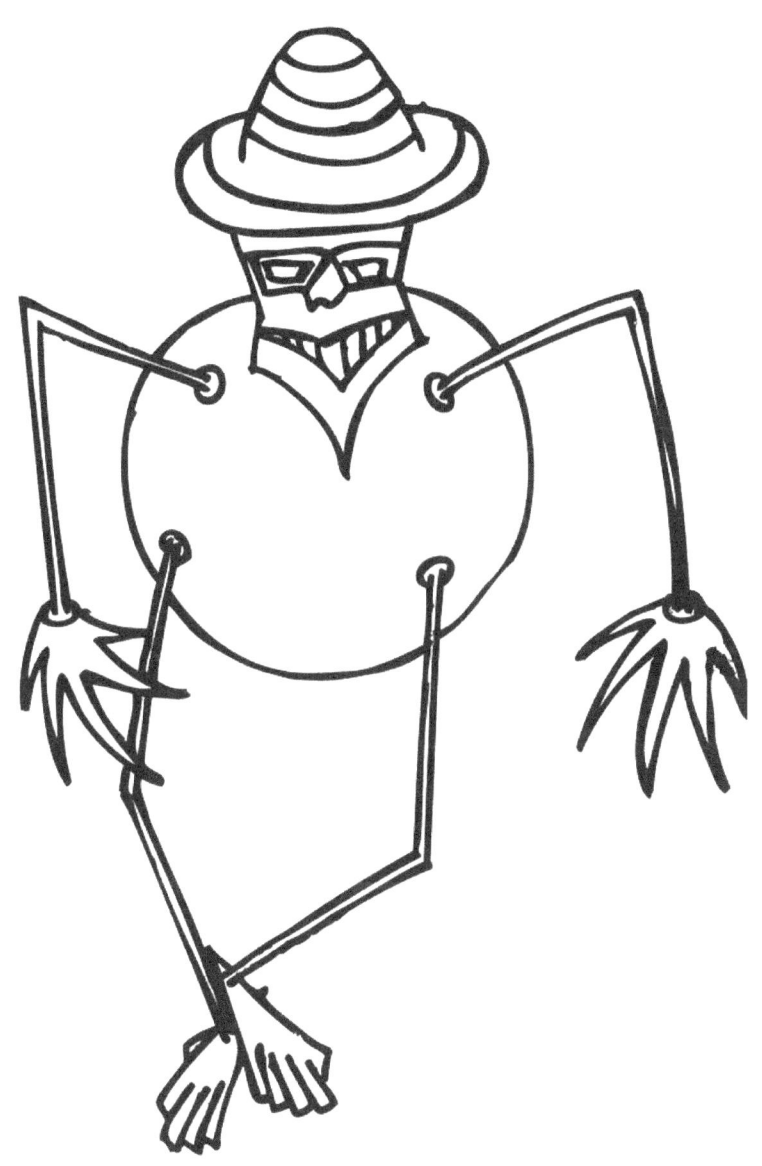

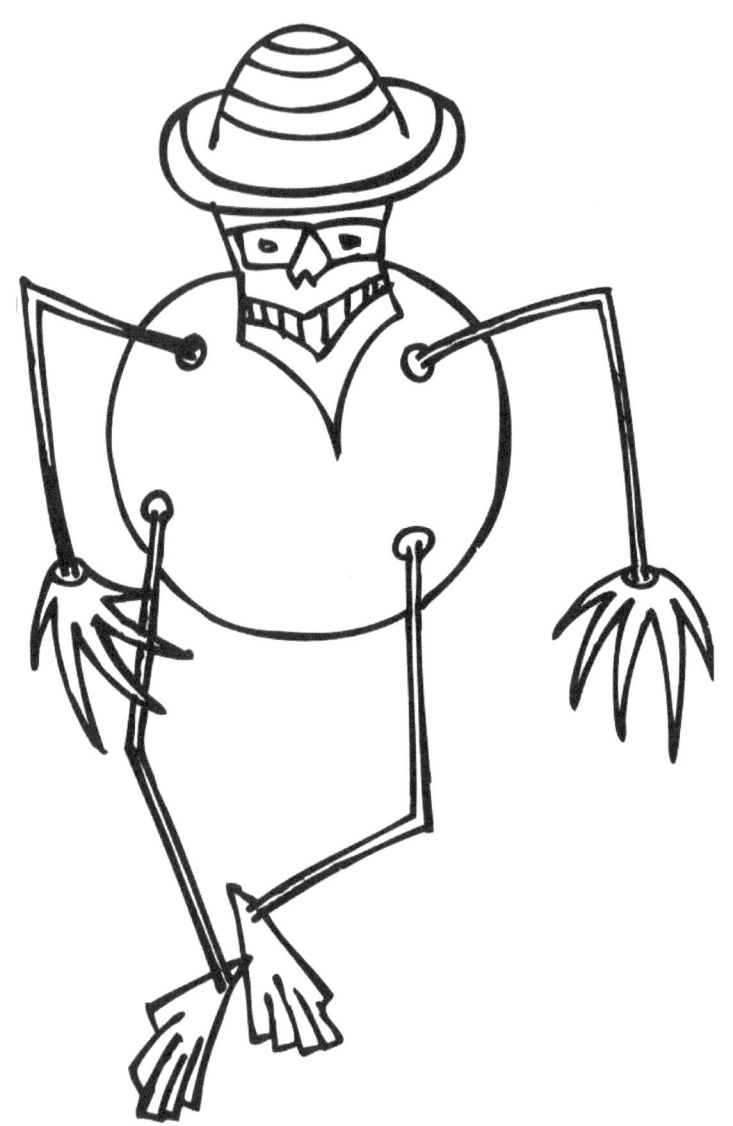